1 introductory series to the modern arts

what is modern

architecture?

n.y. **museum of modern art, new york**

acknowledgments

WHAT IS MODERN ARCHITECTURE? is the first publication of the *Introductory Series to the Modern Arts*. As other volumes are added, this series will eventually form a comprehensive introduction to various phases of modern art. In each case a special school edition will be published. This will be unbound and perforated for use in loose-leaf folders, so that subsequent issues of the series may be added.

This booklet is based upon a circulating exhibition prepared by the Museum's former Curator of Architecture, John McAndrew, and Elizabeth Mock. The text and photographic material of the exhibition were revised under the editorship of Margaret Miller.

Special acknowledgment is due the following photographers for their generosity in permitting the use of their photographs:

Walter Boychuk, R. T. Dooner, Hedrich-Blessing Studio, F. S. Lincoln, Roy E. Petersen, Ezra Stoller, Roger Sturtevant, Philip N. Wallace.

The Museum also wishes to thank the *Architectural Forum* for permission to reproduce several plans which have appeared in past issues of that magazine.

Victor D'Amico
Director of the Educational Program

contents

CORRECTIONS

Page 8. Column 1, line 10, for "below" read "above."
Page 16. Column 1, line 6 of paragraph 3, for "at the right" read "below."
Page 16. Column 2, line 1 of paragraph 2, for "above" read "below."

our buildings are different from those of the past
because we live in a different world

what is modern architecture?

During the last hundred years our environment has been dramatically transformed, largely by Science. Not only has science altered our ideas of comfort and convenience, but even of time and space, and of the relation of man to man and to the community.

the modern architect is a scientist

Science has likewise reshaped our architecture. To provide for the many changing needs of modern life, architecture must meet many new practical problems, and must depend on the scientific point of view in solving them.

The modern scientist does not rely on guesswork, nor on the acceptance of what someone else may have thought, but on **analysis**; **test** and **proof**.

And similarly, the modern architect studies his problems in an **analytic** spirit. Not content with secondhand solutions, nor with habitual repetition of old forms and technics, he works out many new ones, **testing** them and **proving** their value.

and a psychologist

Science can help the architect make his buildings as efficient as a modern machine. The brilliant French architect, Le Corbusier, once said: *A house is a machine for living in.*

This is, of course, true of a good modern house, but the good modern architect must give his clients something more than just an efficient machine; he must give them an enjoyable place in which to live and bring up their children.

The architect must have the human insight necessary to construct an architectural environment which will be psychologically pleasing to his clients, as well as the scientific knowledge capable of providing for their physical well-being.

and an artist

Architecture is an art, moreover, and while it makes good use of science it is not **subservient** to it. Science can guarantee the durability and practical usefulness of a building, but only the creative imagination of the architect can give it beauty.

but most contemporary architects are not modern

Every great past age has had its own style of building, a natural expression of its time, but ninety-nine per cent of the buildings built today are **not modern**. For unlike the scientists, most architects of the last hundred years have not sought the most direct solutions of their problems, but have borrowed past styles from their libraries; their minds have all too often been like magpies' nests full of stolen trimmings; their buildings ape the work of times and places not our own.

The modern architect is not homesick for the past and its buildings, but welcomes the stimulating challenge of the present we all live in, and welcomes also our efficient new ways of building.

Within the last twenty years an authentic new architecture has taken root in many countries. Though there are natural variations because of the differences in daily life, in climate and in local building materials, these thousands of modern buildings show the new, healthy spirit. Their architects, sometimes without being aware of it, have shared a common point of view, fresh and vigorous.

What are the foundations of this new architecture?

5

part I

2000 years ago the roman
architect VITRUVIUS said:

ARCHITECTURE should

meet three requirements

utility, strength, beauty

Let us consider these three ancient touchstones for they are still valid today.

utility

FORM FOLLOWS FUNCTION has become a maxim of modern architecture. For the modern architect makes conscientiously sure that a building will serve its particular purpose well and assume the architectural form most advantageous to its use.

Straightforward expression of function often results in buildings of a new appearance. We live differently from our grandparents, and we do not build for the same purposes. Therefore our buildings, if honest, will not look like theirs.

new types have been evolved

The skyscraper office building (Pl. 1)* grew up in our crowded cities along with big business, which tended to concentrate in small areas. High land values made it desirable to increase rental space, and the buildings themselves proved excellent advertising. The first skyscrapers were built only sixty years ago.

The mammoth department store, now familiar everywhere, was nonexistent eighty years ago. For the convenience of the modern shopper dozens of stores have been brought under one roof and one management (Pl. 2).

The large apartment house, too, is a recent development (Pl. 3). With modern construction it is cheaper to build one fifty-family apartment building than fifty private houses. Not only are rents therefore lower, but housekeeping itself is easier and cheaper.

All three are new problems for the architect. If he plans for efficient usefulness, and lets the forms evolve naturally from functions, his buildings will resemble no architecture of the past; their forms will be new because their functions are. Thus the way we live is the basis of our new architecture.

* NOTE: For complete identification of plates in part I see list of illustrations on p. 35.

1

2

3

4

5

old types have been restudied

The house has taken on a new form because our everyday life has changed and demands a suitable new setting.

We like rooms which are simple and easy to care for (Pl. 4). We like to open our many windows day and night to welcome the fresh air which our ancestors apprehensively avoided (even by pulling curtains around their beds).

But many people have imitations of old interiors, like the bedroom below (Pl. 5), and thus foolishly preserve many of the old disadvantages.

Many other familiar types of buildings have been transformed. This school (Pl. 6), for instance, is arranged for the many varied activities of the school today, radically different from the strict and limited routine of a few years ago. The open plan provides maximum air, sun, light and privacy for the main building and the eight separate classrooms.

But the school in Plate 7 is typical of many non-modern schools built today. Here modern activities are squeezed into a rigidly conventional architectural formula designed to enhance the prestige of the community rather than to serve the physical and psychological needs of the children. The imitation-colonial exterior is like a badly fitting slip-cover.

6

7

specialized use

Sometimes a special use leads to a novel form. The accordion-like walls and ceiling of this auditorium resulted from acoustical calculations to prevent echo (Pl. 8).

equipment

Once only five per cent of the total cost, now often thirty-five per cent, mechanical equipment can affect the appearance of a building. Modern central heating makes a house warm and comfortable even if pleasantly opened for light and view (Pl. 9). Rooms need not be box-like compartments, but can flow freely into each other.

New inventions often break down old limitations. The congestion of cities made skyscrapers expedient; the steel skeleton made them possible; but it took elevators to make them usable (Pl. 10).

site

Sympathetic attention to site — ground slope, rocks and trees, sun, wind and view—may affect the design of a building as much as any consideration of function. In this house (Pl. 11), bedrooms are on the lower floor, living rooms placed above to enjoy the view and the adjacent garden.

large-scale planning

Even the finest building, whether skyscraper or house, is of little value if it must be squeezed into the cramped streets of already over-crowded cities. Our entire environment—our cities, our towns, even our countryside—needs drastic redesigning in terms of fitness for modern life. Thus the decisive importance of our great public works: low-cost housing, parkway systems, irrigation projects. These are problems which must be tackled with bold imagination and careful coordination of planning and construction if both practical and humanly congenial architectural forms are to result.

strength

new construction

In modern architecture **strength** is no longer synonymous with massiveness, for more efficient new structural materials are now used in forms scientifically calculated to avoid waste.

12 Traditional masonry construction relies for its strength on thick supporting walls. Now, however, walls are frequently non-structural: they merely serve to keep out the weather or to subdivide interior space. Their supporting function is taken over by a light cage-like skeleton of steel or reinforced concrete. Instead of hiding this framework under heavy masonry façades, the modern architect designs exteriors which reveal the true character of the construction, and plans interiors to take advantage of the possibilities of freely placed walls.

The STEEL SKELETON, developed in Chicago only sixty years ago, is one of the most drastic revolutions in the history of architectural construction. Easily and quickly erected, it is now usual for large building in this country (Pl. 12).

REINFORCED CONCRETE is made by pouring concrete over steel rods laid in temporary wooden molds. The concrete hardens to form a jointless, solid mass, strengthened by the embedded steel. This material is suited to **13** skeleton construction, but its fluidity is used to better advantage in flowing or slablike forms (Pl. 13).

Both steel and reinforced concrete are well adapted to CANTILEVER CONSTRUCTION. A cantilever is simply an overhang, or the projection of horizontal beams or slabs beyond their points of support.

old construction

Often, however, traditional kinds of construction (such as the stone or brick wall, or the wood house frame) are employed because they still **14** serve their purpose as well as they ever did (Pl. 14).

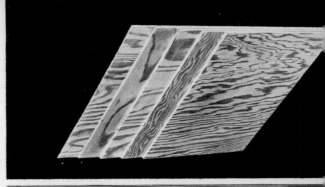

new materials

Along with new structural systems, many new materials have been scientifically developed to make buildings stronger, cheaper and more comfortable. The wealth of efficient and handsome materials a modern architect can command would astound an architect of an earlier age. For example:

PLYWOOD retains most of the structural virtues of ordinary boards, and to them adds several new ones. It is built up, sandwich-like, of thin layers of wood glued together with the grain of each layer at right angles to that of adjacent layers (Pl. 15). This gives new strength and greatly reduces warping.

Manufactured in large sheets and usable indoors or out, it is well adapted to prefabricated construction (Pl. 16). Each panel of this house consists of a sheet of plywood glued on either side of a light wood frame. Since the resulting panels are self-supporting, they are easily and quickly assembled into walls, floors and roof. No conventional house frame is necessary to hold them in place.

GLASS BLOCK is most suitably used as a wall which admits light, yet excludes cold, heat, glare and noise (Pl. 17). More than any other new material, glass bock has been stupidly misused as a "modern" mannerism with disregard for its practical advantages.

old materials

Old materials are often used in new and ingenious ways, sometimes in the traditional way. Or an old use may be borrowed to serve a new purpose. This openwork brick wall on the terrace of an Italian hospital (Pl. 18) is derived from the openwork walls used to ventilate barns in northern Italy.

beauty

As the preceding pages have shown, the modern architect is guided by the demands of **utility** and **strength**. The fulfillment of these requirements will produce an honest building, but it will not automatically assure a beautiful one. For the style and distinction of a modern building depend finally upon its **design**. It is here that an architect works as an artist, continually exercising his discernment, his imagination and his sense of beauty. Through this process of design building becomes architecture.

Let us look at some of the elements of modern architectural design.

the open plan and new space

The new spaciousness which the open plan gives a building is among the most important innovations in modern design. The open plan is often facilitated by modern construction which gives the architect great freedom in placing walls.

A house with an open plan differs from a house with a traditional plan in the arrangement of the main living space: instead of being cut up into box-like rooms, it is one free-flowing space. Hall, dining and general living spaces are all parts of one compound volume, designed for different uses.

Standing inside, one enjoys a pleasant feeling of expansive openness; and as one moves about, one sees new vistas from one part through to another (Pls. 20-23). Scarcely interrupted by the great areas of glass, inner space seems to flow on outdoors to fuse with the immeasurable space of nature.

The continuous and fluid quality of space in modern architecture is unlike the handling of space in any architecture of the past, and can be one of the most distinctive and enjoyable elements of a modern building.

12

1   Hall space
2   Dining space
3   General living space
4   Bedroom
5   Bath
6   Kitchen
7   Servant's room

Steel skeleton with freely placed walls. All the main living space is open. Only bedroom, bath, kitchen and servant's room are isolated.

19

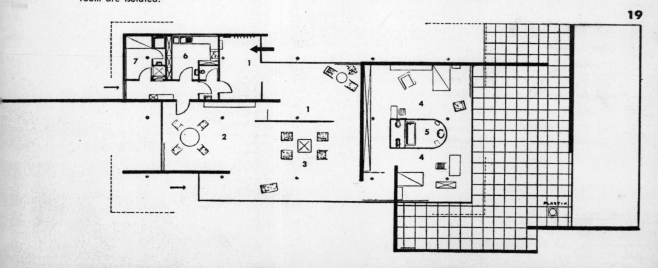

20

21

22

23

24

25

14

volume instead of mass

This new emphasis upon volume affects not only the plan, but also the whole form of the building. Modern exteriors are designed as light, enclosed volumes rather than heavy masses.

In older architecture the massive supporting walls were often emphasized by deep-set windows and doors (Pl. 24). In modern architecture, the walls usually appear to be thin, surface planes enclosing the interior space of the building (Pl. 25).

Much of the beauty of a modern building depends upon the broad, continuous sweep of flat exterior walls. This effect is often facilitated by the smooth perfection of machine-finished materials and enhanced through the deliberate and purposeful use of **repetition** (Pl. 26).

This can be most clearly seen in the arrangement of windows: they are often boldly repeated over a whole wall, sometimes in an allover pattern, sometimes in horizontal or vertical stripes, continuous or broken. Frequently they are concentrated in large areas of glass.

26

27

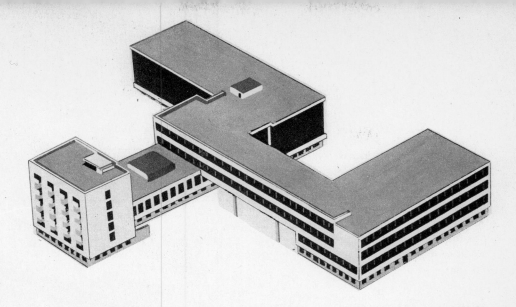

28

asymmetry

A building which must provide for many varied activities, like this technical school (Pl. 28), may be divided into several different parts of various sizes and shapes. If they are arranged for efficient use they will not fall into a rigidly balanced symmetrical scheme, but will assume a freer asymmetrical form. Similarly, the arrangement of the doors and windows will usually be asymmetrical.

This does not mean that the final composition need be undisciplined or unbalanced. With his plain walls and window arrangements of continuous or broken stripes, bands or allover patterns, the architect can meet any of the functional demands of the interior. By strategically adjusting the proportions, he can logically and sensitively relate each wall to the next and achieve a coherent, harmonious organization of the whole building (Pl. 29). The balance is not so obvious as in a symmetrical scheme in which everything matches on either side of an axis. It is a more subtle, asymmetric balance.

The forms of modern architecture are more severe than those of past styles. But by arranging his plain walls, plain doors and plain windows in adroit off-center balance the expert architect can give his designs great variety and freshness. Simple forms can be used eloquently.

15

29

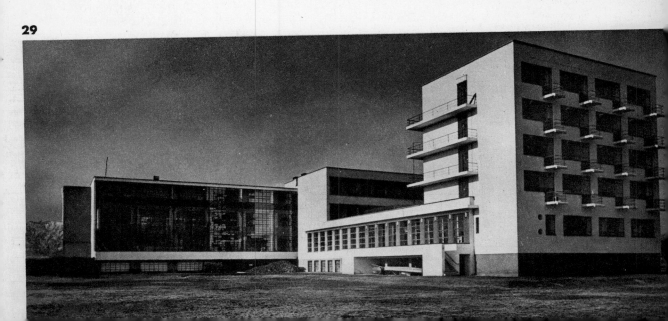

absence of ornament

Traditional architectural ornament was made by master stonecutters. In the modern world the craftsman has been replaced by the machine. As yet no acceptable machine-made ornament has been made. Therefore ornament of the traditional kind finds no place on a modern building.

structural forms can be ornamental

The interest, variety and accent which ornament gave traditional buildings are now provided by other means. For example, the actual structure of a building, wholly or partially revealed, may itself make a striking and appropriate pattern (Pl. 30).

Many trusses and columns developed by engineers for purely practical purposes have surprising beauty. The architect may use these forms or he may invent new ones based on the same structural principles, like the reinforced concrete columns at the right. This row of powerful, finely balanced columns (Pl. 31), enhanced by a glossy surfacing, is more beautiful to modern eyes than if it had been a richly ornamented, classical colonnade.

Or the architect may transform a simple ancient support like the wooden post by applying an engineer's ingenuity to a rustic material. The projecting wooden fins which give these loggia columns their subtly swelling contour also serve to reinforce the slender pole against lateral bending (Pl. 32).

Both of the columns above are the work of the same architects; both vividly express the unique structural virtues and individual beauty of two widely different materials.

16

31

32

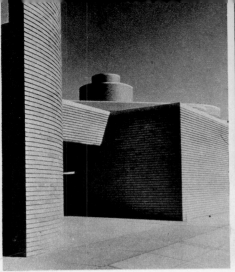

33   34

In a style without ornament proportions and shapes must be very carefully studied, colors and textures sensitively related.

use of abstract forms

Like many modern painters and sculptors modern architects admire the severe beauty of abstract forms. The precision of modern construction allows the architect to reveal harmoniously proportioned rectangles or smooth cylinders in their full perfection and purity (Pl. 33).

Sometimes these elementary geometric forms are contrasted with more complex shapes of a freely curving abstract character. In this dining room (Pl. 34) the curved wall and the circular dance floor set off the fanciful jigsaw shape suspended from the ceiling.

materials instead of ornament

For further interest and variety the architect relies upon the texture, color and pattern of the many materials at his disposal.

Some architects like to exploit the sleekness of glass, chromium and other highly polished "machine age" textures in designs of new technical elegance (Pl. 35).

In recent years architects have come more and more to delight in the richer, more varied surfaces of wood, brick and stone, materials as old as architecture itself (Pl. 36).

17

35   36

free forms of nature

The architect likes to relate his design to the ever fresh variety of the free forms of nature. He often uses plants as a decorative element in his unornamented rooms, sometimes singly or often over a whole wall. Or he makes the view through a glass window-wall become part of a room, like a living scenic wallpaper (Pl. 37).

In recent years architects have been particularly concerned with achieving a sympathetic alliance between a building and its natural setting, whether by subtle contrast or by more intimate harmony (Pl. 38).

Above all the modern architect wishes to transmute the practical into the beautiful. In this he does not greatly differ from the great builders of the past. But today our practical demands have changed and our ideas of beauty have changed with time, as they always do. A living architecture will embody our new attitudes toward the world we live in.

37

In looking at old and modern buildings, consider first whether the architect has satisfied the reasonable demands of **utility** and **strength,** and then see if he has gone beyond this to create, through his design, architectural **beauty.**

38

part II

examples by

Frank Lloyd Wright

"Fallingwater," country lodge for Edgar Kaufmann, Bear Run, Pennsylvania, 1937 (Guest house, 1939).

This famous house, one of the masterpieces of American architecture, is so intimately related to its fine site that architecture here becomes inseparably united with nature. The weight-bearing walls, made of the same stone as the ledges on which they stand, are built of long, split rocks laid in an irregular pattern which recalls the stratification of the stone ledges themselves. The cantilevered balconies of reinforced concrete which carry the main living space out over the stream and provide sun terraces at either side and above echo again the lines of these ledges. Though the construction and whole conception of the house are bold, a majestic serenity is achieved.

Connected to the main house by a bridge and covered walk, the smaller simpler building on the hill above provides guest quarters and garage (Pl. 41). Here, as in the main house, the overhang assures pleasant diffused light in the glass-walled rooms.

39

41

42

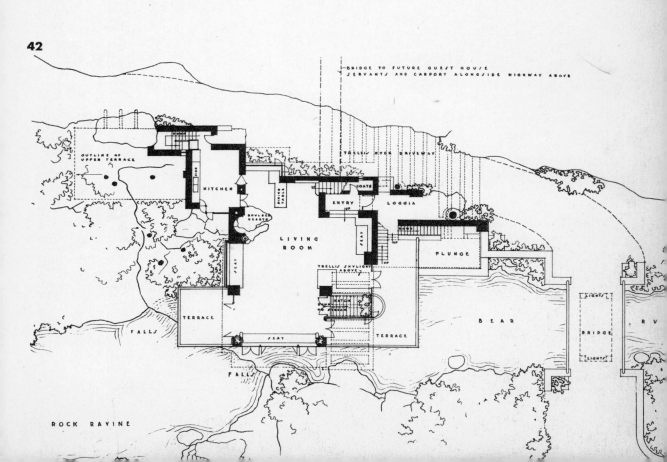

BRIDGE TO FUTURE GUEST HOUSE
SERVANTS AND CARPORT ALONGSIDE HIGHWAY ABOVE

OUTLINE OF
UPPER TERRACE

TRELLIS OVER DRIVEWAY

KITCHEN

COATS

ENTRY
UP

LOGGIA

BOULDER
HEARTH

LIVING
ROOM

SEAT

SEAT

PLUNGE

TRELLIS SKYLIGHT
ABOVE

TERRACE

BEAR

SEAT

BRIDGE

TERRACE

FALLS

LIGHTS

LIGHTS

R V

FALL

ROCK RAVINE

43

44

Carl S. Koch, Jr.

Own house, Belmont, Massachusetts, 1940.

One of a group of five inexpensive houses planned and built together on a steep hillside overlooking Boston, this house also contains the office of its owner-architect.

Built against a rocky ledge, the house is literally invaded by nature. From the entrance a stair curves down the rocks past a great plant-window to the living room (Pl. 46), where the magnificent view is exploited by windows running the full length of the room (Pl. 43). Beneath the living room is the office (Pl. 47) where the rock is again exposed, this time forming an entire wall.

The romantic attitude evident in this interpenetration of house and nature, and in the sensitive use of natural materials, stone and unpainted wood, has in no way interfered with function, comfort and economy. The amazingly low cost of the house is largely due to its compact rectangular plan, its simple details.

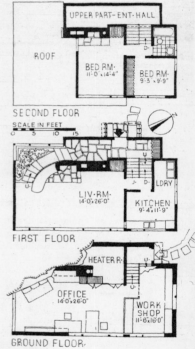

SECOND FLOOR

SCALE IN FEET

FIRST FLOOR

45 GROUND FLOOR.

46

47

48

49

John Funk

Heckendorf House, Modesto, California, 1939.

More good modern architecture is found in California than anywhere else in the United States. Especially fine are the simple wooden houses, part of California's long tradition of straightforward wood construction. This house is typical, yet distinguished by a natural elegance of line and detail.

The design is well adapted to a difficult site and a hot, dry climate. Since the street lies to the south, the house was set back in its lot and shielded from the street by a sunny fenced-in garden.

A five-foot roof overhang protects the long glass front from too much direct sunshine. The boundary between the interior space of the house and the open space of the sheltered garden is minimized by the transparent wall. Projecting trellises and climbing vines further emphasize the close, informal relationship between house and garden. **50**

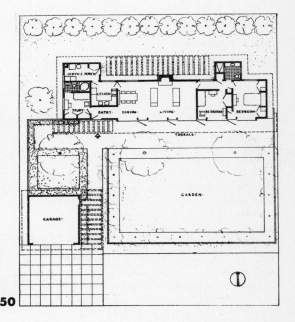

23

51

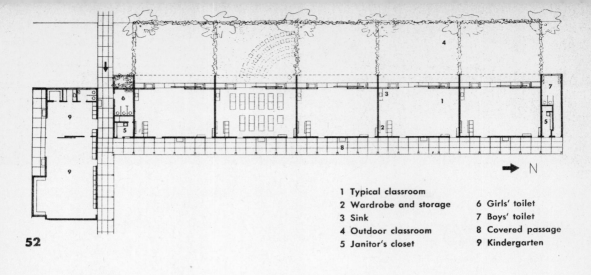

52

1 Typical classroom
2 Wardrobe and storage
3 Sink
4 Outdoor classroom
5 Janitor's closet

6 Girls' toilet
7 Boys' toilet
8 Covered passage
9 Kindergarten

Richard J. Neutra

Bell Experimental School, Los Angeles, California, 1935.

Modern education, with its emphasis on "learning by doing" and its concern with the physical and psychological well-being of the child, demands a completely new type of school, designed not as a pompous public monument, but as a healthy, pleasantly encouraging background for the child's activities.

This light wood-frame building, an addition to an older school, takes full advantage of California climate. Class-rooms were planned in a one-story row to give each room its own outdoor class area, immediately accessible through sliding glass doors. The long glass wall is protected by a deep roof overhang and adjustable canvas blinds. An open corridor connects the classrooms.

The construction was carefully calculated for earthquake safety, economy and easy expansion.

54

Eliel and Eero Saarinen;
Perkins, Wheeler and Will

Crow Island School, Winnetka, Illinois, 1940.

Instead of designing an imposing façade and then ranging the classrooms behind it as best they could, the architects of this elementary public school first worked closely with the faculty to plan a model self-contained classroom, ideal in its efficiency and in its expression of the famous Winnetka philosophy of education. The classroom, sketched in Plate 55, then became the basic unit of the complete design. The main entrance of the school is shown in Plate 54.

This typical classroom is a projecting bay (Pl. 56), with windows on two sides, and bright with sunlight and color.

Movable furniture permits the room to be used for many different activities (Pl. 57). It has its own workroom and lavatory (Pl. 55), and its own play-yard with pet house and garden.

Educational buildings today are not nearly so progressive as education itself. We need thousands of new schools, north and south, in city and country, with the gay informality, the childlike scale, the flexibility and the grateful acceptance of the outdoors which characterize the schools on these two pages.

25

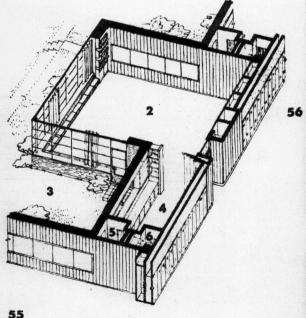

55

1 Corridor
2 Classroom
3 Outdoor play space
4 Workroom
5 Toilet
6 Closet

56

57

Le Corbusier and Jeanneret

Swiss Dormitory, Paris, 1930-32.

Highly organized simplicity of plan and dramatic clarity of composition make this dormitory for Swiss university students in Paris one of the most distinguished works of the great Swiss-French architect, Le Corbusier.

The building has three distinct elements, each decisive in outline yet planned in harmonious relationship to the whole: (1) an irregular single-story unit containing entrance hall, dining facilities, etc., (2) a curved stair tower and (3) an elevated block of students' rooms. The steel frame of the dormitory block was raised on concrete columns to provide a sheltered terrace beneath (Pl. 61). The south front is entirely glass to allow generous light to the rows of rooms behind (Pl. 60).

In the freely curving rough stone wall of the dining hall (see plan and Pl. 59), Le Corbusier gave impetus to the recent tendency in modern architecture toward more fluid planning and increased use of natural materials.

26

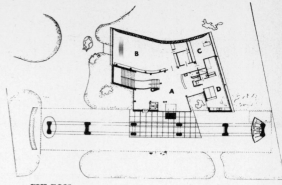

FIRST FLOOR

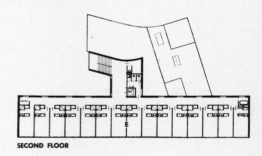

58

SECOND FLOOR

A   Hall
B   Dining hall   D   Janitor's quarters
C   Director's office   E   Bedrooms

59

60

27

61

62

63

Walter Gropius

The Bauhaus, Dessau, Germany, 1926.

Gropius was founder and director, as well as architect, of this famous art and technical school. Here new methods of education were developed, based on the principles of modern art and the need for appropriate designs for machine production. The Bauhaus building was itself a clear statement of many of these revolutionary ideas.

The airview (Pl. 62) shows how the parts of the building are sharply defined according to use and arranged in a free, pinwheel-like composition. Classrooms (1), craft workshops (2) and studio dormitories (3) are connected by auditorium-dining hall, offices, etc. The floor and roof of the workshop wing are cantilevered out beyond the reinforced concrete supporting frame (Pl. 64). The walls become glass curtains, defined at the top and bottom by apparently floating bands of white stucco. The effect of weightless transparency is one possible only in modern architecture.

64

65

66

Brinkman and Van der Vlugt

Van Nelle Factory, Rotterdam, Holland, 1927-28.

Another architectural masterpiece of the twenties is this Dutch tobacco factory of reinforced concrete and glass. "Mushroom-headed" columns and slablike floors were poured together to become a single monolithic unit. This method of building, radically different from traditional post-and-beam construction, is possible only in reinforced concrete.

With nothing to support, the walls (like those of the Bauhaus workshops) become merely a protective shell, glazed or opaque as required (Pl. 65). Continuous bands of glass provide the even light desirable in a factory interior.

Clean and daring in conception, precise and elegant in execution, this building is an excellent example of the arrangement of simple regular parts in a lively, asymmetrical composition.

67

68

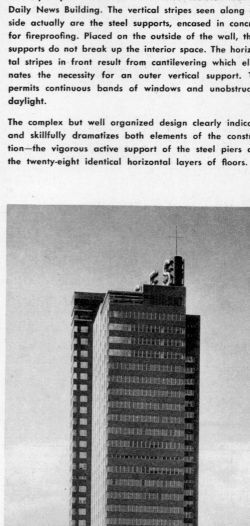

69

Howe and Lescaze

Philadelphia Savings Fund Society Building, Philadelphia, Pennsylvania, 1931.

This skyscraper reveals more of its steel skeleton than the Daily News Building. The vertical stripes seen along one side actually are the steel supports, encased in concrete for fireproofing. Placed on the outside of the wall, these supports do not break up the interior space. The horizontal stripes in front result from cantilevering which eliminates the necessity for an outer vertical support. This permits continuous bands of windows and unobstructed daylight.

The complex but well organized design clearly indicates and skillfully dramatizes both elements of the construction—the vigorous active support of the steel piers and the twenty-eight identical horizontal layers of floors.

Raymond M. Hood and
John Mead Howells

Daily News Building, New York, 1930.

Like many skyscrapers, this one dramatizes its verticality.

The long white vertical stripes are emphasized by the dark stripes between them made by the windows and the panels of brown brick. The horizontal steel members supporting the floors are not expressed in the design; one does not notice where they cross behind the dark and light stripes. This pattern conceals the full character of the steel frame which holds up both the floors and the external shell of dark and light brick. Yet the design is simple and effective and makes good use of the setbacks demanded by the New York Zoning Law.

70

Alvar and Aino Aalto

Finnish Building, World's Fair, Paris, 1937.

An architectural problem peculiar to the industrial age has been the exposition building, with its requirements of structural lightness, economy and arresting novelty. Plaster palaces can never be the real answer. When architects have recognized that these same limitations, if frankly handled, can become an advantageous basis for free and imaginative design, they have frequently produced admirable buildings which have decisively influenced the course of architectural development.

Such a design was the Finnish Building at the 1937 Paris World's Fair, with its strongly personal, yet beautifully logical, use of wood—Finland's chief product. The photograph above shows the vertical ribbed boarding of the exterior, the reinforced wooden posts (see also Pls. 71 and 72) and the quadruple reed-bound columns which support the inviting man-scaled entrance loggia (Pl. 70). A forest of vine-clad poles enlivens the central court (Pl. 73). This delight in revealing the character of natural materials, exceptional in 1937, has since become an important part of contemporary architecture.

71

72

73

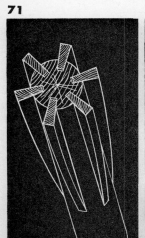

Farm Security Administration

BURTON D. CAIRNS and VERNON DEMARS, architects.
Farm Workers' Community, Yuba City, California, 1940.

Of all our low-cost housing projects, those of the Farm Security Administration have most often succeeded in being economical, livable and architecturally distinguished. Their Yuba City community is shown in the foreground of the airview above. The informal rhythmic arrangement of the house-rows about a magnificent pecan grove contrasts pleasantly with the rigid hexagonal layout of the adjacent camp for migratory workers.

The houses are designed for a maximum of comfort in a region of mild winters and hot summers. Instead of windows the sleeping floor has two rows of flaps, the lower of plywood, the upper of translucent glass substitute (Pls. 75 and 76). The south sides of the house-rows are protected from rain and summer sun by an emphatic roof overhang and by the projection of the second story over the first. Faced with silver gray asbestos cement boards, the long rectangle of the upper story seems to hover lightly over the dark unpainted redwood below.

With its easily flowing site plan, its respect for climate, its long low lines and its use of native redwood, this community is an excellent example of our newly regained concern for the relationship between architecture and its natural surroundings.

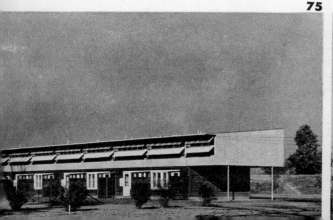

Tennessee Valley Authority

ROLAND A. WANK, Principal Architect.
THEODORE C. PARKER, Chief Engineer.
Dam and Powerhouse, Hiwassee, Tennessee, 1940.

Modern architects owe much to the work of the engineer. The unconscious beauty of strictly utilitarian structures such as grain elevators has long been admired, and the engineer's development of new materials and building techniques has influenced modern architecture in many ways. Architects have often been called in to "dress up" a bridge or dam or industrial building which engineers have designed. Yet true collaboration of architect and engineer is rare.

Like hundreds of other structures, large and small, built by the TVA since 1933, the dam and powerhouse at Hiwassee are the successful result of such collaboration. The simple form of the powerhouse is in quiet contrast to the monumental dam rising above it. The same material—reinforced concrete—is used for both structures, but the powerhouse walls were given scale and texture by the rough-sawn wooden molds into which they were poured.

The sober beauty of the huge dam itself entitles it to rank with the aqueducts and bridges which have been admired since Roman days.

Lubetkin and Tecton

Penguin Pool, London Zoo, 1933.

34

Like all truly modern buildings, this pool was carefully designed for its purpose: to keep the penguins healthy and happy, and to display to visitors all the talents of these comic birds.

The steps at the top of the ramp (Pl. 79) are penguin steps, made the right size for the way they walk. The ramp leads to the shallow pool where, through a glass wall, people can watch the quick graceful movements of the birds in the water.

The oval pool with its screen wall and daringly light, curved ramps was developed directly out of the properties of the material used—reinforced concrete. The construction photograph shows the reinforcing rods in place preparatory to the pouring of the concrete (Pl. 79).

In this structure, so modern in its purpose, construction and design, we find complete fulfillment of the 2000 year old standards of Vitruvius: utility, strength and beauty.

list of illustrations

53. Bell Experimental School. Outdoor classroom. Photo Luchhaus, courtesy of the architect.
54. ELIEL and EERO SAARINEN; PERKINS, WHEELER and WILL. Crow Island School, Winnetka, Ill., 1940. Exterior. Photo Hedrich-Blessing.
55. Crow Island School. Isometric view of classroom unit. Courtesy of the *Architectural Forum*.
56. Crow Island School. Classroom bays. Photo Hedrich-Blessing.
57. Crow Island School. Classroom. Photo Hedrich-Blessing.
58. LE CORBUSIER and JEANNERET: Swiss Dormitory, Paris, 1930-32. Plan.
59. Swiss Dormitory. North façade.
60. Swiss Dormitory. South façade. Drawing.
61. Swiss Dormitory. Terrace.
62. WALTER GROPIUS: Bauhaus, Dessau, Germany, 1926. Airview.
63. Bauhaus. Exterior.
64. Bauhaus. Workshop and technical school.
65. BRINKMAN and VAN DER VLUGT: Van Nelle Factory, Rotterdam, Holland, 1927-28. In construction.
66. Van Nelle Factory. Rear façade.
67. Van Nelle Factory. View from street.
68. RAYMOND M. HOOD and JOHN MEAD HOWELLS: Daily News Building, New York, 1930. Photo courtesy of the *Daily News*.

69. HOWE and LESCAZE: Philadelphia Savings Fund Society Building, Philadelphia, Pa., 1931.. Photo Dooner.
70. ALVAR and AINO AALTO: Finnish Building, World's Fair, Paris, 1937. Entrance.
71. Finnish Building. Diagram of reinforced wood columns. From the *Architectural Review*, Sept. 1937.
72. Finnish Building. Loggia.
73. Finnish Building. Central Court.
74. FARM SECURITY ADMINISTRATION: Burton D. Cairns and Vernon Demars, architects: Farm Workers' Community, Yuba City, Calif., 1940. Airview. Photo courtesy of FSA.
75. Farm Workers' Community, Yuba City. House-rows, south side. Photo Lee, courtesy of FSA.
76. Farm Workers' Community, Yuba City. Photo Lee, courtesy of FSA.
77. TENNESSEE VALLEY AUTHORITY: Roland A. Wank, Principal Architect; Theodore C. Parker, Chief Engineer. Dam and Powerhouse, Hiwassee, Tenn., 1940. Photo courtesy of TVA.
78. LUBETKIN and TECTON: Penguin Pool, London Zoo, 1933.
79. Penguin Pool. In construction.
80. Penguin Pool. Photo Lincoln.

36

10,000 copies of this book have been printed in August, 1942, for the Trustees of the Museum of Modern Art by the Photogravure and Color Company, New York. The type was set by the Publishers Printing Company, William Bradford Press.

1   171 -1)